A JOURNEY OF PERSPECTIVE

A Journey of

PERPSECTIVE

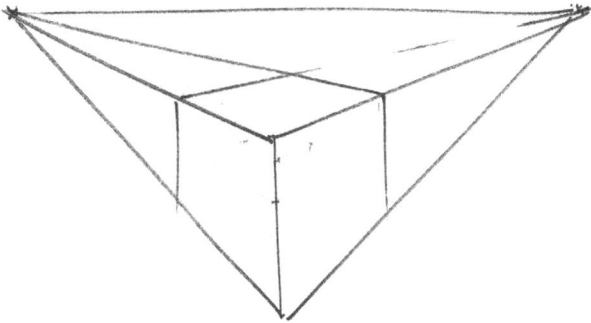

D U N E   S T E W A R T

Published by Dune Stewart

Book Design by Kory Kirby

Illustrations by Kaitlyn Hebden

Cover Artwork by Ramelyn Ballon

ISBN 978-1-7351015-0-7

Printed in the United States of America

For Nancy Stewart *(Nana)*

C O N T E N T S

PART THREE: RESTORATION 51

INTRODUCTION

I began this book during a dark period of my life and used writing to find myself again. I found that it has helped me clear my head and grow into a more open-minded person. I created this collection to demonstrate that no matter how bad you are feeling, there is hope, even if you can't yet see it.

It took me a long time to come to terms with many aspects of my own identity, and I find myself learning more with each day that passes. I have learned about my priorities and what I want for my life. Looking back on these poems, I found that with persistence and the clear determination not to be depressed anymore, your path is made. You may feel that you are off the path and are searching for your way back, but just know that being lost is also a sign that you are already on the path.

This book was written over the course of a ten-month period, but it contains stories from over a decade ago.

Just know that although time may seem long, it will stitch itself together to make sense in the end.

This book is for all those who have suffered and for those who are currently suffering. I hope you can find hope in what feels like a roller coaster ride of emotions, even when you are blind to the next loop in the journey.

part one

DETERIORATION

Untold Stories

This book

An open wound stitched together by endurance,
Concealed information bridged with ink on paper,
These untold stories
Are now open and free.

They cannot hold me down like they used to.
I face them head on with my "I Don't Give a Fuck" attitude.

Leaving behind doubts and fear,
Pursuing goals with unconditional love.

These stories
Many have been laid onto paper like it is my will,
And by that I mean

It is a toil of emotions condensed into a frame of paper.

These stories
Most of them read like a newspaper,
Skimmed for highlights and left to be caught by the wind,
Where whispers of words only graze the ear of a bystander
And are then stomped on by another.

These stories
Are not all that has happened

They are but a glance into the mind,
Left aching to tell more,
But that is saved for another time,
For this is written not by the mind,
But from the soul.

Turning Tides

Each page turned
Is a scar that took months to heal,
But you turn away as if it is a story you have heard before.

But this time,
If you take your time,
You might just realize how often each page is read and reread in my mind.

I Am Not a Photographer

Visions of stories escape my mind and land on paper.
Other times, they are captured in still images,
But I am not a photographer,
I am a storyteller.

Give me a camera, paintbrush, or pencil, and I will show you a story.
Captivating ideas strike with a burst of joy,
But only for a first initial shock.

The rest is snapshot convenience—
Messages with no story.

Therefore,
I am not a photographer.
At least . . .
Not the one I want to be.

Hours, days, weeks, and now months,
I pace the small square footage of a bedroom,
Only to be trapped in an overthinking state,
Which makes me look psychopathic,
But I'll find the answers I'm looking for eventually,
Right?

Desperate to tell stories,
I find my old, true love,
Poetry.

Like a soft kiss that comforts and compels,
Not rejecting any opinions,
Allowing freedom of expression and no judgment,
My true art form.

A Callout to the Inner Artist

I can't seem to find the paintbrush that will let me paint myself
and not someone else.

I try to take a photo, but it comes out more like a thoughtless
snapshot than a reflection of my heart.

I try to draw, but the pencil acts as if its #2 branding is its
permanent stature.

I attempt color theory and leave with only appreciation for black.

I find inspiration in the joy of life, but create almost imminent
darkness.

Lost within the movement of time--insomniac creation,

Attending school is the only way to keep myself motivated.

Writing poetry is the only concept I can grasp [right now].

Do You Know Poetry?

No, I mean like,
Do you KNOW poetry?

Because I wanted to know if you heard the screams in the tones,
The claws that ate the wall for its entire three-course meal,
And the ache sounding like a small whisper of air.

Witness the small space that people try to fit themselves into,
Even though they can just tear a bigger hole for themselves.
Throw them a lighter
So it's easier to spot what lies beyond.

The layers of hurt or pain that have gathered to keep out any hope,
Trying to guide the mind to conjure good thoughts,
Which is hard when all around you is complete darkness,
Lurking thoughts of ignorant advice from those who don't have a clue.
They're being foolish
-Letting people walk away with contrived beliefs.

Mood Swings

I love life, man,
We are living our best lives right now,
And we are not going to let anything get us down!

But what if it doesn't work out?
Am I ever gonna be good enough?
Does anyone even care what I do?

Haha!
I'm doing great though!
My career's taking off like a plane,
Leaving my weighted-down friends at home
So I can live for myself.

Why do I feel sad now?
What the fuck?
Oh my god,
I want to stick my fist through the wall
Even if you just look at me dirty

Or . . .
Oh my god!
Stop coughing!
It's so annoying!
Ahhhh!!

But you ask, "How you doing?"

"I'm chillin'."

That's what you want to hear, I'm assuming.

To the Bone

A Toast to the Neglected Body I Leave Behind

Be thin,
Be beautiful,
Be pure.

Carving out the flesh that forms me,
Leaving sticks and bones,
An exoskeleton figure I'd love to see.

Thin.
Beautiful.
Pure.

What It Is like Having Dermatophagia

Dermatophagia is a compulsion disorder of gnawing or biting one's own skin, most commonly at the fingers.

A subtle mental disorder that arrives in the unconscious mind,
A forceful one-way attraction with no brakes.

(bite)

Usually stemming from high anxiety and depression side effects,
Leaving me indefinitely calm and collected,

(bite)

Because my subconscious found a way to relieve anxiety with no pain . . .

-to others-

An easy fix, right?

A quick pick-me-

(bite)

up

(bite)

Like that last pill that cured that one made-up disease,

Yeah I know it,

(rip)   *(gnaw)*

I don't take it,

(rip)

Because at least I know this is a sane state of mind,

Unlike what some drugs can do to people,

(bleed more)   *(bleed(maybe))*

And how it can do nothing to them and still somehow be hurtful.

Being left as a conscious zombie to *fight your disease*.

(scar)

That's the sad part of the problem,

(callouses)

The feeling of knowing the action of biting is always existent and
that it can always become a habit again,

(heal)

But that also means getting better does as well . . .
Right?

(bite)

Saying Goodbye

For Nana

On my aunt's couch,
Nine-something at night.

Memory of watching movies with my cousin before falling asleep,
Being awoken by a tall figure,
Blurry vision sharpens but only after my ear catches a note.

Hearing "C'mon let's go."
Exiting the house to pitch darkness,
Entering the car, a bright white light behind me,
As if a metaphor for future distress.

Slow rise to ten miles per hour exiting the cul-de-sac,
And then with a blunt and mumble-tone voice,
I was told she was gone.

No immediate reaction,
Just stared out the window
Until a single tear reached the bottom of my chin.

I held my composure the entire ride.
Slow deep breaths and quivering lips,
Rolling my eyes to prevent more tears,
A sudden stop in time to reminisce.

Smell of Baskin Robbin's cappuccino drink fills my nostrils,
Essence of cigarette smoke fills the air,
Hearing phrases she used to say,
Feeling the comfort and support of a mother figure.

Indescribable loss and feeling of emptiness,
Feeling so much only to be left with no feeling at all,
A dark departure into a lonely abyss,
Where you find yourself lost in shadows.
Others tell you how to react,
but they never cure your grief.

The day we lost a mother,
And celebrated a birthday.
The day we lost the core of our childhood,
The day we found ourselves missing the glue that held us together.

The year that I got promoted,
The year my cousin got promoted,
The year my sister graduated,
And she was not a witness.

The person who raised seven grandkids,
The person who tutored all of us,
The person who'd take care of us at least five days a week,
The person whose goal was to make us all happy,
The hero who accomplished her goal.

Who died from cancer.
The hero we all still feel in our presence today.

Vicious Cycles

Cringing from the pain of my stomach ache,
Breathless from the missing heartbeats,
I smoke to forget,
Cry from random waves of sadness,
And smoke again to forget.

To me, this is just another story,
Another effect of a dark past event.
A great turmoil means a great story,
And that is what I chose to live for.

I am a writer,
I am a storyteller,
I am a painless soul dancing in the wind of avoidance that keeps me sane.
I am not a survivor nor a victim,
But a witness to a storm brewing,
With the mist of the water hitting my face through the window.

I can choose to shut the window,
But then who will hear the voices in the distance,
Crying out for refuge as the storm approaches?

Lost Brother

For Kirby, who I always thought of as a brother.

I felt weird when I found myself forgetting
How to miss somebody,
Anybody.

As if others' existence was
irrelevant, Then you left.

Your unknown

departure- My still

frame.

Boarding ticket in hand.

Boarding gate closed.

Hoping it'd open up once again.

It didn't though-
And that's probably what hurts more,
Knowing that returning is no longer a choice.

Sorry, I Wasn't Brought Up Like That

No, sorry,
I didn't watch *DragonBall Z* or *Pokémon*,
I didn't learn about cars and sports,
I wasn't into lifting weights,
I didn't listen to whatever music you were probably into,
I didn't spend my time chasing girls,
or playing with their hearts.

But I did watch *PowerPuff Girls* and *Totally Spies*,
I did learn about love and heartbreak,
I was taught how to treat a woman,
I was into writing and dance,
I listened to the upbeat lyrical notes that boomed on my Walkman,
I spent my time sitting at a table with an ashtray in front of me,
Waiting to hear the next story I'd hear from my favorite person,

Then I found myself dissociating from the scene when I walked away
from my seat,
Like I'd be back,
And afterwards,
I just spent my time chasing the memory I'd lost.

So, no-
I can't relate to the trending topics of the male experience,
For I wasn't brought up listening to the mainstream media,
And I was too distracted by my favorite person
To even give them the light of day.

Matter of fact,
It could have been night time for all I knew.

Time Capsule

For all of us who grew up together.

He was just a boy who played with his cousins, and everyone would
laugh and run.
The smell of summer air so fresh and the daylight so bright.
Some would jump over the rose garden and get injured by the thorns,
Sprinting toward the pool to make a splash into the next childhood game,
Then heading to the right side of the backyard wall to find two naked
people sun bathing,
Then sprint into the middle of the yard where they would collect
Easter eggs,
Then make their last stop in the left corner to cheat at Hide-N-Seek,
Climb the wall to freedom from exposure,
Dodging the crosshairs of keen eyesight,
Then leaping back when they got to the front street.
Then they would get tired and head inside because of the summer heat,
Get a snack of strawberries sprinkled with sugar,
Then head to the garage to make a unique sight,
Shooting spitballs at the popcorn ceiling,
Then sliding down a slide with a plastic turtle shell as a sled,
Until it was time to visit the dead,
And leave ghosts in the graveyard for everyone to find.
One would scream,
All the rest would run like laser beams,
Leaving all of them out of breath.
They'd rest on the couch,
Watching *Thirteen Ghosts, CatDog,* or *Blue's Clues,*
Drifting off to sleep,
Waking up to their parents' arrival.
Leave for the night,
And then wait for it to repeat.
For without each other,
They felt incomplete.

Under the Fog in a Cloud of Rainbows

For you.

Table for two,
Under a string of lights that caress the peak of our shelter-
That which shades her face,
Hazel-light-bluish eyes that seep into my brain like a flashback on
a projector, Creating nothing but smiles for me,
Wanting a Polaroid to treasure-you.

A still image of what has happened and what could be,
But never will be.
-An authentic feeling

Hair lays like silk fabric,
Everflowing with the shine that compliments her face,
Red lipstick that flares off her face like a neon sign in city streets.
I love her.

I always have.

As Time Has Passed

I had always wondered if you still thought of me-
About how it used to be;
Stellar.

Who Am I?

Sitting in my car, I drown out my reality.
Solitude in the driver's seat comforts me more than any friend I've had,
But it's okay because it's not their fault.

Shutting down friend requests like spam mail in my junk folder,
I'm not sympathetic,
I wreak havoc.

My presence is as blunt and harsh as morning coffee thrown on your face;
I am not kind.
I am a borrowed soul. I recycle my fake personality to conform to society;
I am not me.

Memories of an 8-year-old ghost I wish I could summon to my rescue,
To distill the calmness in my mind,
A settle to the disturbance.

But that's not reality.

The reality is
I am a newly recycled energy source.
My defects are like a tumor—
Minor but dangerous.

I am not here.
I am not present.
I am not me.

I am
(trying to be)
A photographer,
A writer,
A film enthusiast,
A lost soul just trying to find the burnt out light in the forest
of what once was.

I am not asking for help.

I feel independent.
Stubborn and foolish,
But a lone wolf with no pack to call home.
Gravitating to the usual comfort of movies and TV, I am not lonely.
This is my new *normal*.

I'm Just Tired

I'm not mad,
I'm just tired

Tired of hearing bickering from couples in relationships, then being
told, "It's just how we talk,"
Tired of seeing political protests when we can easily come up with
a compromise,
Tired of believing I am the only one who doesn't love myself,
Tired of trying to find happiness like I will find it if I just peek
around the corner of the block,
Tired of screaming internally from anger and irritability,
Tired of hearing "thoughts and prayers," when thoughts and prayers
do nothing,
Tired of having false hopes when I know they just lead to disappointment,
Tired of faking a sense of purpose when I am more lost than ever.
Tired of not having passion for the career I love and want anymore,
Carrying the soul of perseverance with a hopeless mind;
Skilled-Heartless Results.

Tired of having to write these emotions down like it is my will,
Tired of feeling severe anxiety every second of every day,
Tired of running away from my present, as if the future will always
hold more,
Tired of not making decisions for myself, letting others take the
wheel . . .

But mostly,

I'm tired of just feeling tired.

(Im)perfections

Taking quotes from people's past mistakes,
I leave no room for error
Due to their trust.

But my realization of unique struggles
Causes backlash,
Forming advice to cliché,
Left with nothing but my own trusting thoughts,
Leaving trust only to yourself and nobody else.

When you leave the door closed for too long,
Advice becomes criticism,
Criticism yields cynicism,
Blocking all that is meant to keep you--

Going.

O-Side

To the O-Side fam

The beautiful breeze of another Saturday morning,
Smell of a blueberry blunt aborning,
Heeding to the trending beats of humbling music,
In the midst of April,
Then head out to join the locals.

Hop in the car,
Windows down,
Low-riders around,
Think they're the cool cats in town,
But they're not slick,
Easy to pick,
Scanning the area while we hotbox this bitch.

Chillin' in the parking garage,
Then eat at Teri's,
Ordering that D1 plate,
Then leaving to thrift,
Or stop by the old work,
Since we all chill during what's supposed to be a graveyard shift.

Barely making those bills,
Rent is as high as it is in Beverly Hills,
It's expensive as fuck,
So I dipped,
So I wouldn't get stuck,
But you best believe I'm coming back,
With a career that takes off like Fleetwood Mac.

Beach vibes every day,
Since you can't afford to do much else except pray
Pray for that life,
Because many get taken,
Just ask anyone who's a native,
They probably can name each district that's regulated.

26 - A JOURNEY OF PERSPECTIVE

I remember just living there within a year,
I saw more than just a few lives get taken,
Like sure, it's a great place to live,
But you better carry a pocket knife,
Because you are about to learn O-Side's way of life.

Be treacherous and be cautious,
Party hard and sulk in the sun,
Before you get brought down from a Thompson machine gun.
Just kidding
That's too out in the open,
Gotta be discreet,
Keep it OG,
Grab the knife,

Because tweekers can be creepers.

But I love the city,
Keeps you on your feet,
Go out at night,
Feel the hype,
Have a date on the beach,
Literally . . .
But it could also be a figure of speech.

Head over to MiraCosta and get an education,
Run into the most amazing artists,
To keep your concentration,
Feel challenged,
Then get a degree for that harsh life of reality.

Rollin on that 5,
But I'm in dead-stop traffic,
Going downtown gonna take longer than the forty-minute express,
But nevertheless,
I just put on some good tunes,
And try to enjoy another O-Side afternoon.

Feeling on the Magic

Stage 1: Giggles
I laughed so hard, my emotions ran free.

Stage 2: Harmful Poison
My stomach ache lasted 15 minutes, and, fuck,
The bloating had me slouched in my car seat.

Stage 3: Adventure in City Lights
Illumination,
Soft admiration,
Like a train light passing through the tunnel,
Like a cliffside mountain view.

Stage 4: Ego Trip
Now here's the tricky part-
As my id breaks open, I pass into full consciousness,
Gazing over events that laid beyond me,
Like an ecstasy of dreams curving into my face at ninety miles per hour,
I lost my identity.
~~As a human~~

Stage 5: Space
Lost my shit,
World spiraling into a Saturn ring left unknown to its own end,
A shake ache while awake,
Then . . .
Beautiful meditation music I heard aloud,
Envisioning the beauty of rebirth and self-reflection.

Stage 6: Lost in Space
Lost my shit.
Again.
Worried?
Yeah, very worried.
Woke like a bear getting his hide chewed on,
Anxiety slammed me against the ceiling,
Left me sinking into the bed, swallowing the darkness that surrounded me.
I just kept shaking.
And shaking,

And shaking,
And shaking.
Then I got warm.
The soft, comforting covers slide against my arm.
I ease into the warmth as the clock spirals.

Stage 7: Parallel Universe
I am awake,
But am I awake?
Or is this like another dream,
Or is my dream now my
reality,
Or has my reality always been a dream and this is the rush of
realization of my true identity?

Am I just losing my mind?

Is the emptiness and fullness in life I felt just an hour ago
The feeling you receive when it is all over?
Just a gust of wind that flies by, only swaying you to its musical
notes?
Just for a brief moment to know
Everything will be fine,
And the universe has your back?

In My Dream

Awaken to soft brown eyes so clear,
Filling the space like I have sunk into a flower bed
Of my own dreams.

You,
Dancing in a white dress in the middle of our one-bedroom apartment
To the music of birds chirping in the sunshine on the windowsill,
Overlooking the fire escape of the 25th floor to see the city.

Hovering over you as you write your next piece,
Hanging our first collaborative piece of art on the wall,
Then looking back and reminding ourselves how we fell in love,
Later falling to the floor, talking about the future and what it
holds for us.

Cooking breakfast together because that's the only way I choose to learn,
Feeding each other as if opposite hands attract,
Brushing your hair out of your face to see the beam of beauty.

Saying good evening as "buonasera"
Because Italian makes us sound so much sexier,
And smiling every time you laugh,
Because it sounds like the vitality of life.

So here's a toast-

To the life that gives me purpose,
To the girl who makes this dream come true every day.

Whoever you may be-

Purpose of a False Prophet

Staring down the road of the unknown,
And glancing behind me at goals I've already met,
I become conscious of the journey itself.
Stuck in the tracks with both shoelaces tied together,
I find myself lost without purpose.

The kind of thing you are driven to do,
The kind of thing that makes you happy,
That one reason to keep waking up.

Please don't worry,
I'm not "bad" anymore,
But having strength with no goal,
Is just as detrimental as the opposite.

Post-depression is like coming out of a forest
With nothing but your senses to keep you on track,
Completely lost in the tracks of the mud,
Only knowing what is above you.

I drink a lot of coffee now,
Because it is the only thing that stimulates me anymore,
With a blunt nearby to cloud my mind and shut out the voices that
neglect my wishes and worth.

The sad part is my happiness is a lot like my nausea:
It comes in waves just long enough for me to feel it,
Then it goes away like I didn't deserve it.

Mortalidad

Líneas borrosas entre realidad y fantasía,
Pregunta de falta de cordura o cierto del desacuerdo,
Ignorancia es felicidad tomado alegremente,
Ahora . . .
Mi mantra.

Escuchamos a otros sobre espíritus,
Y encuentro que ellos son correcto:
El oscuridad es fácil para tragar porque es nuevo para la mayoría.
Como un ex miembro de el oscuro,
Yo puedo decir,
Procede con precaución,
Porque . . .
Demonios son cambiaformas.

Mis demonios son mi pasado,
Pero mi futuro es lleno con luz.
Fragmentos de mi autorretrato roto en el espejo,
Cada día yo ponlos lentamente de nuevo juntos.

Mortality

Blurred lines between reality and fantasy,
Question lack of sanity or dark truth,
Ignorance is bliss taken lightly,
Now . . .
My mantra.

Listening to others about spirits,
I found that they are correct:
The darkness is easy to swallow because it's new to the majority.
As an ex-member of the dark,
I can say,
Proceed with caution,
Because . . .
Demons are shapeshifters.

My demons are my past,
But my future is lit with light.
Fragments of my self-portrait broken in the mirror.
Every day I put them slowly back together.

My Daily Cup

First cup of coffee in the morning is the best,
Not as good as the second.
But depending on the mood of the day,
There could be a third,
And if I get bored,
Why not a fourth?

Aw man,
Too much cream and sugar,
I gotta wake up-
A fifth should do it!

But I want to write more,
Stay focused.
Forget Adderall,
That's dangerous!
Why risk getting a pill addiction
When I can just have another espresso!?

Well, it's late now,
I want to slow down,
So I mix my half cup,
With what's left over from a half ounce,
Put on my headphones,
Drown into music,
But now my stomach hurts,
Maybe I should eat,
Oh, but it's already midnight,
I don't want to make it worse.

So I lose ten pounds,
Have sleepless nights,
Forget I feel weak,
Always ready to put up a fight,
Strive and stride,
Side by side with all my friends,
One sees the lack of appetite,
And asks "Are you alright?"

Memory Loss

But you can't leave-
I need someone to tell me the great memories in life.

Musical Companionship

Rap was the best thing that happened,
Opened my door up to explain situations,
Both perspectives and relations.

First it started with some new-school rapping,
Then I quickly learned it turned into mumble discussing,
Then I went back to the roots,
Discovered *Juicy* and other hit songs,
Listened to 2Pac on my way to work,
Then Lyrics,
Who used powerful, bilingual language that mattered.

Discussing police brutality and political matters,
I was looking for good content with great flow.
That's when I went back to Eminem,
and learned how to write content with my pen,
Listening to Rap God to learn his flow.

And then we got to rap beat instrumentals
That's when I started free-styling,
Then expressing myself freely.

I was not a rapper, but I spoke what I felt.
That is when I discovered my true self.

Accepting the Truth

Depression is neither the truth nor a lie,
But an honest reaction from life's hardships.
The solution?
Acceptance.

Not of your unhappiness,
But of life for what it is-
An ever-fluid, consistent motion of emotions,
Which you will either accept or disregard.

Positive perception will attract positive thoughts;
Negative perception will attract negative thoughts.

Looking to get better?
Think wiser.

The Door to Emotion

Walking up to an abandoned house,
I knock on the door,
But nobody answers.

I turn my thumb ever so slightly on the doorknob,
Leaving the creak of the door to make my presence known.

As I enter,
A faint memory reaches out to me from the darkness.
It gasps for attention, but I leave it, suffering.

I glance into each passing room,
Witnessing past events that made me anew.
Sometimes I'm finding myself static,
Enchanted by memories that I wish could last forever.
But they will never be real again.
Other recollections stare back, hoping to engulf me.

But there is no light without darkness,
And there is no darkness without light,

Understanding this-we push through to the end.

The Secret Behind How to Take Risks

It doesn't have to be a big, grand gesture.
You don't need confidence.
You will have fear,
And you will not regret it.

It's not a matter of how big or how small,
But rather a realization and acceptance of time.

This is the key to making life fulfilling:
Knowing there's a time limit
And too many dreams to fulfill before the hourglass disintegrates
into the sands of time.
The bedtime story will come to an end,
And still may never begin,
But how does it start off?

By reading the thing,
So by following this logic,
The key to taking risks . . .

Is just doing them.

The Hardest Part of Life

Traveling through time with only hope and anguish,
Hearing stories of success and pleasure,
Leaving darkness with no near sign of light,
Hoping the glimmer of light finds me like a city I've been waiting
to see for the first time.

I'm ready for that fresh feeling of opportunity and growth.

Struggling with finances and taking risks for the future,
Entering the unknown only to stop somewhere in the journey,
Realizing success came easier than you'd thought.

But a determination to become happier
Takes more effort than getting a bull back in its cage.

There's only two paths to take:
One to success,
Another to dream.
It is time to fix your problems.
Take it and own it.

References

"Hey, I just heard this great song!"
"Oh, that reminds me of this one song!"

Will you leave your decisions to others' ambitions and interests,
And not to your personal taste?
Conform like the suits you wear to the office?
Listening to the songs on the radio?
Staying updated on cultural trends?
Or will you go against the trend
and create a new thread?

To say that nothing is original anymore
Is to say that any reference is superior due to its age,
That your thought is not invalid,
But just a new rendition of an older thought,
A redefined structure with new flaws,
An antique polished to a modern standard.

Fascination

Fascination with death, because it's a friend who I can trust to act when called. Fascination with the life, because I'd rather find meaning,
Answering my identity and purpose,
Than to live ignorantly,
Letting life slide by
Without any recollection as to why it passed in the first place.

Fascination with personal struggles-
So I make them for myself.
Fascination with past events that become lessons learned,
Fascination with the unknown future, slowly opening its hand like a blossom in spring,
Fascination with what it holds in its palm, with what it offers me.
Facing the future feels like entering a museum that doesn't allow flash photography: Minimally intimidating, but with some slickness,
You can get by just fine.

Fascination with the rap group *Year of the Ox*, because they're talking about what matters in the world,
The issues we avoid as a public,
And writing a few pitches for solutions,
Guiding us on a tour of reality with no pit stops,
Because there is so much going on that we avoid because it doesn't affect us,
So stop hiding behind the transparent curtain that you think will keep you safe,
And look out for one another next time.

I'd Rather Have Something Than Nothing

A call to the wind asking which way it was blowing,
Asking others why they choose to live the way they live.
Many will talk about the details of downfalls, and how being lost in
the darkness is a hole we think we can never escape,
When in fact, if you continue on,
You may someday find the light winking in the distance-

Finding that missing piece that may be worth living for.

Because our self-worth is like the US government's treatment of its
people,
We want to tear our image from the mirror.

So if you have a dream,
Act on it,
Make yourself happy.
If we spend our lives how others want us to,
Then will we ever live the life we envisioned for ourselves?

Along the way,
Take care and keep gratitude,
For although you live your life the way you want to,
Not everyone is so lucky.

Expectations

An insincere apology to the expectations that weren't met.
A celebration for the story that was made.

Sorry to disappoint,
But I did not turn out like the average male,
More like an alien that can't be explained,
Only felt.

Dear Mr. Keating

In Memory of Robin Williams

O Captain! My Captain!
I sit in the back-right corner of a room on an early December morning.
The soft sunlight peeks at my face,
And I feel the fresh glacier breeze tapping me on the
shoulder.
As I sit in the brick-layered school,
I turn to face my curious acquaintance,
an invisible spirit of guidance.

He is welcoming and smiling, supportive of my endeavors.
He promotes creativity and revolts against old traditions.
He makes me think outside of the box we are encouraged to stay
trapped within.

He is an entity of lesser known power,
Containing a wealth of knowledge waiting to be unlocked.
He opens all doors to those who are willing to try.

He tells me to strive to greater lengths, to go beyond what I imagined,
Leaving doubts and fears to the stories I write, but not the stories
I live.
What was once a fresh wound
Has now healed into a battle scar of fortitude.

This entity takes the form of a human,
Harnessing legendary characteristics,
Introducing new ways of teaching,
Humorous and captivating.
He was you, Mr. Keating.
Thank you.

Ode to Tig

At first sight,
I thought I was right.
Caught up in the commotion,
My emotions went through their motions.
My depression dug deep inside of me.
There was no light.

I spent days comparing my life to others
Until I came across another who had it harder:
My favorite comedian, Tig Notaro.

A woman who has gone through so much
In just a matter of months.
She first got pneumonia.
Man, we all wished that was it,
But then it turned into C-Diff.
Not many people know this rare intestinal disease,
And there was more terrible news that no one had foreseen.
She got a call from her step-father.
Her mother had fallen,
And then it hit harder:
Her mother was dying, and could no longer talk to her
daughter.

She lay next to her mother,
Left alone overnight,
Capturing her mother's last breath,
Having to say goodbye–

And just when you thought it was over,
Fate threw a couple more smacks towards her.
Her life events were so overwhelming,
It caught the attention of her girlfriend who left,
And couldn't handle the problems that came their way.
So that was the left hook that fate delivered
But there was still one fist coming for her.
Breast cancer.
That was the final hit,
And not in just one breast, but both.

After a double mastectomy,
She found herself being referred to as Sir,
Because of her illness.

But she fought and fought
And hit remission.
And here's the best part:
She married the woman of her dreams
And now they have kids-
Two twins.

Art 21

A website to discover amazing artists,
Where most left me in awe with their originality and exquisite
execution,
Yet I am left aching for more discovery.

Observing and unearthing artists once unknown to me,
Matriculating self-exploration through the visuals of Alex Currie,
Narrating legends like "The Drifter" from Lieke Romeijn,
Using vacancy and isolation as a way to connect like Brendon Burton,
Remembering life's simplest pleasures, captured by Josh Nice,
Or studying how Chrissie White used color theory in "Madison Park
at Night."

While also respecting the artists whose artistic abilities have
transformed them into something divine:

Charlotte Navio's work makes the texture of paint as fluid and
beautiful as any landscape,
And Do Ho Suh's massive designs transport me to his South Korean home.
Yayoi Kusama's polka dot rooms immerse us in her mind,
While Aneta Ivanova displays how emotional self-portraits can open
our own world.
Haruka Sakaguchi's "Original New Yorkers" stands up for the natives
of a city whose culture is being renovated.

.   .   .

To the historic legends that all of us look up to for further
inspiration:

Diane Arbus, who sheds light on marginalized people left in the shadows.
Henry Cartier-Bresson, who challenges our perspective when viewing
street life. Ansel Adams, who presents beautiful scenery in black
and white.
Francesca Woodman, who creates the correlation between appearance
and disappearance in space.
Yousuf Karsh, who illustrates pure emotion from spontaneous interactions
with his subject.

. . .

To of course, my personal favorites:

<u>Robert Mapplethorpe</u>, demonstrating how important topics will not be let go, <u>Erwin Olaf</u>, producing images that reflect our past traditions, <u>Gregory Crewdson</u>, exhibiting that the space can be as big as we wish, <u>Andrew Kearns</u>, who showed why it is important to have great friendships, <u>Brooke Shaden</u>, who made a living out of finding beauty in darkness.

And lastly,
To the artist who introduced me to what it was like to discover new artists everyday:

<u>Anna O'Cain</u>, who teaches us to embrace our unique vision and hone in on our goal.

The Slut and the Falcon I

For Emma Watson and Stephen Chbosky

The effect you ended with is the same you began with.
I am speechless from awe,
You give light to those who feel alone,
Spreading kindness because you understand the hurt,
Reaching out to give a hand instead of receiving one.

You are the change in the world,
And although there is a finite number of people you will affect,
I can proudly say it will double with my help.

I think we both needed to hear you say,
"We accept the love we think we deserve."
Without your words,
A new road would become an under-construction off-ramp,
And delay would be inevitable.

All I can say is, thank you
For letting me visit the island of misfits.
I truly left feeling like one of you.

part three

RESTORATION

The Slut and the Falcon II

For Ezra Miller

So much energy,
So vibrant and full of life,
The grin of a joker,
But I see nothing but sincerity.

Your eyes squint when you smile,
To let me know you truly are living a happy life,
From owning the dance floor,
To owning who you are.
I now find repose when others choose to reject me for who I am,
Not in relationships,
Because I think we can both agree that most are subpar,
But in friendships.

So I just want to say-

Dear friend,
I have been thinking about what you have meant to me.
I have been thinking back to that summer morning and those cold winter
nights, Remembering the question that you once posed,
And I have found an answer:
You are what makes me feel infinite.

Dear Friend

I wish you knew how much I relate to you,
And how when I am in trouble,
You are the first person I lean on,
Because you offer only support and not
Judgement.

I hope you don't think I'm a scam for copying that one guy who had
this idea,
I just find it so compelling how you can speak to me without using
my language. And how each typewriter key I press
Feels like a gust of fresh air,
Where everything I have done wrong,
Has become nothing and the only thing that remains is just us;
Discussing and discovering new characteristics that make our connection
more unique than any relationship,
But then again, every relationship I've seen has just ended in failure
one way or another.
But ours is never unsatisfied, and we work as yin and yang,
not a one-way street that we know will eventually lead us to a dead end.
But hey, even dead ends can have great views,
Especially when you're taught to see how far you've come,
And how far you'll go.

Staying Comfortable

Outside is where you become alive,
Understand how life is to be lived,
Breathing for new scenery,
Your mind clouded only by a cluster of new names,
And not by self-criticism.

Blue sky turns to gray in a new city.
The desert landscape is now filled with green trees reaching towards
the ceiling of the universe.
The edge of town once ended with a freeway, but now it is bordered
only by a blissful river breeze.

Follow the peaks of mountains,
Because if you climb them,
You will understand what you left behind.
On the other side.

There is so much waiting to be seen.

Isolation

My laughter rises from a line laid to paper,
While others' is grounded by their partner.

I am taunted by the beats and lyrics of another story written in
tongues,
While others are captivated by stories of their friend's intoxicated
night,
Until a distraction appears and they forget.

My lessons are delivered by the world's greatest mentors:
Neil Degrasse Tyson, Jim Carrey, Robin Williams, Tim Minchin, and
Alan Watts. Selectively, but fiercely, I engage with their presence
in my life,
Words of wisdom translating to a call to action,
My creations become crumpled papers, overflowing the wire trash can
beside me.
I see others' actions as a stroller crossing yet another square on
the sidewalk that isolates them,
Leaving only room for the physical space,
And nothing for the mind to create.

My inspiration gathers eccentric virtuosity,
With the mundane marooned: a treasure for complacent beings.

My life harnessed the endurance of a runaway train,
Skipping the stops for new arrivals,
Only accepting one-way tickets.

Soaking in the Sun

I used to live in darkness,
But then I discovered life-
A universe of infinite possibilities,
With nowhere else to go but up.

See, if you imagine yourself at rock bottom,
Keep the perception,
Because then it's more than conception,
And has a drive that requires no perfection.

Every decision creates an experience,
So let's live anew.

Words Left Unspoken

Sarcasm has a limit.

If your words turn into a battle cry,
If honesty fails to disarm us,
If we exchange only words of soft hatred,
Then this relationship cannot grow.

If so, don't expect a response.
After all,
We'd already forgotten how to speak to one another.

Helping Yourself

Continuous thoughts rattled into desperate desire for self-discovery,
Seeking comfort in a time of distress,
Until you are pushed like thread through a needle.

Preconceived possible procedures persisting with pathways of painful
paving,
Perspiring palms of panicky perplexity pretending people perceive
passing placebos,
Placing prophecy prominently whilst passing a partly pieced-puzzle
of poisonous patterns,
Promising pursuit until premium proposal of passionate purpose
preventing passiveness.

Stumbling like a stutter in the middle of a reading passage,
Internally clinging onto loved ones' words of hope and resolution,
Only to trigger past emotions and forgotten wounds,
Memories pulling them down until their hand no longer clutches the
rock that makes them rise above.

A sorrowful truth for those seeking reconciliation.

Yet, there is a solution.

Think positive, and let go of negative speculations.
Always look forward, and believe in your future victory.
Take your road step by step,
Walk with patience and endurance.

Don't worry.
Someday you will be home.

Everything Ends up in the Attic

Turn a full 360 degrees and you will find only people glued to their phones.
Glancing into neighbors' windows, you'll find only the light of the TV illuminating the room,
When it should be lit with laughter and tears.

Humanity is lost in a virtual world that leaves us with all the benefits of a voided check,
Thinking we're going to be given valuable information until we unplug,
Finding ourselves,
Once again,
Dissatisfied.

Leaving our feelings to the status updates on social media sites,
Where everybody pretends to give a shit.

Instead we can dive into the story of another,
Laid into the words and images transcribed onto their skin,
Since it is the only tattoo that really claims who they are.

Looking ten to twenty years in the future,
Imagine the life you dream of,
And how you'd like it to be
filled,
Maybe with kids or a spouse,
And now kill it.

Because though we drive towards our future,
We are blinded by our smartphones, which take up so much space.
We only have our peripherals to see the lights that glimmer on side streets,
Leading us down the path of fruition,

And most people will miss the turn.

But if we follow the lights down the street,
If we focus on the future we envisioned,
Leaving no room for technology to interrupt our beautiful lives,
Then we will find ourselves moving into this house which we call home,

Piling boxes in empty rooms,
Ready to fill the space with eagerness,
And when it is all said and done,
We will find all of our material possessions,
Tucked away underneath the light,
With only a view of silhouetted cardboard flaps overlaying one another,
Collecting dust, since everything ends up in the attic.

Shave My Head

Dogs shed their fur, and a new hide appears beneath,
Understanding a new day awaits when the sun arises.

Us, we leave the coat of withered events on our backs,
Carrying baggage until we are released,
Feeling the breath travel through our bodies,
Releasing the tension that weighed us down because of the bricks we
laid.

I feel the tension.

It weighs on my mind like a trash can that was never emptied.
I feel as though my hair is a cover, that I must bare my head to free
my mind of despair,
Scratching my head because my thoughts are racing inside of me,
Which makes me cautious and anxious,
Like carrying a stack of books while not being able to see the stairs
beneath me, Making careful moves that don't lead to a break.

But all I need is a break.

So I gather my thoughts,
I lay them onto paper,
Kind of discombobulated,
But now my mood is modulated.

So if you see a new post of a brand new hairdo,
It is not a sign of despair and tension,
But more so to be a mark of my beautiful ascension.

The Space

Shared space,
Open floor.
Except I'm trapped in the shadows of the corner of the room,
Light seeping through the fabric of my thin-threaded long-sleeve
sweater,
Eyes glimmering and hazy as tears filter my view,
Coward in the depth of darkness,
Until-

Heart bursts out with personality,
Feet slide against the hardwood floors like an eagle gliding over
a lake,
Hands swing into a movement of
Free and full of expression.

Lost in the music inside my head,

I feel free.

Like a gust in the wind with no obstacle to stop its movement.

Dance is the only time our solid shapes become liquid,
A gift of expression so powerful,
It is like reaching the peak of a mountain that overlooks a breathtaking
landscape, And everyone in the audience understands your experience,
A feeling that spreads out of the theater like a wildfire that cannot
be contained.

Straight Men Don't Write Poetry

"Straight men don't write poetry,
That's for homosexuals."

Oh sorry,
I thought I was getting on stage to use the mic because it resembles
a dick,
Except this one spits rhymes and truth,

See, poetry is a way to express your thoughts and your feelings,
So if that means holding the mic is like holding a dick,
Well, shit . . .
I guess I work well with this instrument.

But straight men don't write poetry,
They chop wood and watch football.
They don't express feelings-
That'd be too feminine.

They lift up weights instead of themselves,
Driving a monster truck-
Because we all hate the environment.

But, hey, if poetry is for gay men,
Then that's probably why they're so fabulous,
Ready and free to speak what they think,
Not shadowed by stigma,
Not afraid of what you think.

So call it gay all you want,
But while you sit here frustrated at my remarks,
I gotta ask,
Is it because you are hiding out in the dark-?

Why I Move

Complacency can yield contentment,
but contentment doesn't have to yield complacency.

Arriving in Portland, Surrounded by Trees of Green

These trees are elegant,
Clothed in dresses with rippling skirts,
Swaying and brushing hello to the Earth.

Their branches are like hands reaching out to lost souls,
Connecting them with identity and purpose,
Saying, "Go ahead, and don't be scared."

As you run out into the unknown,
Into the new city,
Into your new perspective,

Solve the soul search,
And clutch onto it with all your might,
Wear it like an amulet that lights the night.

Leap into the hands of faith.
You too shall see the unknown-
It is the next best part of life.

Recovery

My voice has been given a chance to speak out in soul,
Feeling the coping tremble out of my mouth like testimony,
Going places that create nothing but peace in my soul.

With Leon Bridges taking in my soul and releasing its melody,
Year of the Ox proving that rap is not dead and can still be powerful
with lyricism, Lorde producing guilty pleasures that are worth
embracing,
George Yamazawa showing me that there are more great artists to
discover.

Living each day aloof,
No longer despondent,
I feel elated and free,
Where "busy" translates to satisfaction and not disarray.

My mind now rehabilitated, I meditate daily,
Drowning out the thoughts of fears that no longer matter,
And what amazing adventures await,
With whoever is along for the ride.

El Lobo Solitario

Muchos querrán encontrarme,
Pero, no.
Esta es no una descripción para una página (GoFundMe).
No estoy aceptando donaciones,
Y si soy perseguido,
Diré no moleste.

Porque yo soy un viajero,
Solo queriendo ver Islandia y otros países dónde yo pertenezco,
Y tomar fotos que habla a mi alma,
Dónde los paisajes toman y liberan mi aliento,
Y mis zapatos son camaleones,
Cambiando colores mediante los caminos diferentes.

. . .

Dónde yo emerjo como un mejor fotógrafo.

. . .

Fuera de la red,
Dejado en el terreno con lo qué aún está por venir,
Camino con vigilancia y persistencia,
Con sólo dos huellas siguiendo detrás de mí.
Este viaje tiene la naturaleza cantando su música para mis oídos,
Con conexiones girando alrededor del mundo como una mapa de Verizon
Dónde mi solo zonas de itinerancia.
Son los lugares no he llegado todavia.

Lone Wolf

Many will want to find me,
But don't.
This is not a description for a GoFundMe page.
I am not accepting donations,
And if I am sought after,
I will say not to bother me.

Because I am a traveler,
Only wanting to see Iceland and other countries where I belong,
And take photos that speak to my soul,
Where landscapes take and release my breath,
And my shoes are chameleons,
Changing colors through different paths.

. . .

Where I emerge as a better photographer.

. . .

Off the grid,
Left in the terrain with what is yet to come,
Trekking with vigilance and persistence,
With only two footsteps following behind me.
This journey has nature singing its music to my ears,
With connections rotating around the world like a Verizon Map,
Where my only roaming zones,
Are the places I haven't reached yet.

I'm Proud of You

Four words so rare,
They create confusion, for they are never said enough.

Living in a world where greatness is expected,
And anything less than perfect is subpar,
We overlook our strengths and accomplishments,
Leaving the stories of failures to those who follow in our footsteps,
Hoping it leads both of us to victory.

It was a while before I heard these words again,
And the sound was sweeter than honey on bread,
But trust issues led me to question their
authenticity,
Doubting I could be worthy of such praise.

By protecting my mind from outside voices,
I only reinforce my self-destructive personality.
It is an outlook on despair:
Hoping to chase our destiny,
Only to realize
We only needed to hear
Four words so rare,
To know that someone cared.

The Poem I Couldn't Write since There Was Too Much to Admire

To my "vestie" and favorite professor, Amanda Q.

Loving your job so much,
Loving your students more than we know,
Acting more like a teacher than a professor,
Teaching a class where, at the end,
We hope there's another beginning.
Understanding hardships and helping others deal with them,
Showing passion for others' work when yours should clearly be
appreciated as well (Because *American Narcissism* is amazing),
Owning a fashion sense that nobody else can pull off quite as
well,
Taking pride in seeing a student succeed . . .

I can't wait to be just like you.

You have inspired me to become a photography professor.

I am truly grateful and honored to have been mentored by you.

Eight Rules for Life

DO THIS FROM NOW ON:

1. Be nice to EVERYONE.
(We don't know their story.)

2. Unplug from your phone!
(Make valuable friendships/relationships.)

3. Stop EGO TRIPPING (credit to G. Yamazawa on that one).
(Realize you are no better and no worse than anyone on this planet.)

4. Be grateful for everything.
(We have it way better than you think.)

5. Step into the UNKNOWN.
(It is not as scary as it seems.)

6. Stop blaming others for your problems.
(Take some fucking ownership.)

7. Measure success by happiness, not wealth.
(Rich and miserable, or poor and happy are plausible clichés nonetheless)

8. BE HAPPY.

Take Care

Hold each other while you can,
Because time fades and dreams live,
And dreams can create distance,
And although you may seem happy for them,
You will find part of yourself missing as you venture back into your
own world of dreams.
You try to stay connected,
But distance creates mutual dissonance, changing your unique connection,
Leaving you distraught, afraid that your friendship is ending.
But it is okay.

Friends are made around corners.
All you need is a little courage and a will to move,
And when you go to hitchhike on that corner,
Be alert-
You might just get picked up for another amazing ride.

My Little Assistant

To the daughter I hope to have someday.

I can hear your laughter,
I can see your brown reflector-filled eyes,
Brown hair so wavy,
The wind stretches it for miles.
Hugs so tight,
I can't breathe for days.

My favorite series in my portfolio,
My favorite story,
My favorite person.

From running in a field, chasing stars,
To sleeping in a hammock in an abandoned fire lookout;
From our first picture together,
To seeing you do what makes you most happy.

Far-fetched predictions and hopeful adventures,
This life I've imagined for the both of us,
Is only realistic if you are satisfied.

The life you want to live,
I will support.
If you are more practical than artistic,
Don't feel like you disappointed me–
You never can,
Because I will always love you.

Beauty

Beauty is not destroyed by despair.
Your wrinkles are the marks of a life lived,
A story to tell,
A lesson to be passed down,
A memory to encapsulate yourself in.

How Was Your Day?

I ask, "How was your day?"
Because the walls between us don't allow for anything but small talk,
Closed off spaces that leave us detached,
And after a period of waiting,
We get concerned.

Like, what if we fall out of love?
Or what if we don't feel that spark that was there before?
Or what if . . .

We plan for only the now,
And leave the what ifs for our future selves to discover-

Together.

EPILOGUE

Guilty Pleasures

Some will tell you that you need to have certain tastes because of
your gender,
But stereotypes are bullshit-forget them and do you.
We all have something we love,
We just have to look really deep within,
If you see it,
You will feel a glow of light that hazes in the distance,
The exit to this rabbit hole of a dream.

If you can embrace your guilty pleasures,
Then you can embrace who you are.

I show mine like a flag of a person who now uses these to occupy
every space of their mind,
Leaving no room for outside opinions,
In order to be your truest self.

As a consumer to this brain diet,
I found myself succumbing to the ecstasy of happiness,
Where the end of this ride is a waterfall leading off a cliff.
The ride is amazing and joyous,
And some will wonder if it is worth the
latter, But I say yes with all my might.

-That has been on my mind.
Because when we think about that quote,
We think about someone else,
But never ourselves
So, love yourself.

Choose to be happy.
Don't chase it.

A quick lesson that was a big transition to my new perspective on life:
Act on your dreams,
Don't let them sit on the sidelines another day,
Because we can win any day we are alive.
So, go out there and conquer what you deserve.
We all deserve what we all have to give to this beautiful world.

Resurrection

All that is read,
is all that was true,
but with my stories laid to paper,
The scar healed,
And my perception grew.

Great moments will become stories,
Bad moments will become scars,
Only difference is if you will accept it,
Now that you've come so far.

On the Horizon

I used to drown my morning in cups of coffee,
Then leave to work a dead end job-to drink more coffee,
Then smoke during the break,
Come back high,
Then spend the night after my shift smoking more-either with people
or alone in my room,
Then get too high to stay awake by the time I got home.

I now start my mornings with a cup of coffee,
Then leave for the full-time photography job I landed,
Then come home to read-a lot,
Then spend time writing,
And spend time with others,
Then listen to music that refreshes my soul.

And now when I go to bed,
I don't need to smoke so I can sleep.
I stare at the ceiling, thinking of how far I've gotten,
And how far I am about to sprint.

Mixed Race

We are told to love every part of ourselves,
Left to the percentages of our multicultural nationalities,
To define where we stand in this class system of
individuals,
And thankfully mine contained a percentage high enough
To give me a slight pigment in my skin,

That I can't wait to sun bathe in,
So I can pretend it increases my percentage and I can stand with
them more prominently.

The pigment was then transferred to my taste buds,
Loving the spice and the flair that life had to offer,
Giving us a language where the music forces a dance routine,
Where there are moves nobody else can master,
Because they don't have uncontrollable hips.

Tacos you always try to savor but scarf down anyway,
Horchata that works on a hot sunny day,
And champurrado for those cold winter nights.

Being Mexican is one of the few things I take pride in,
But it's unfortunate that I can find the benefits on my other side.

For Hideo Kojima and Thank You Vengeful Mosquito

It wasn't someone close to me that showed me why being independent
was so powerful,
Why speaking your voice and staying true to yourself and your art
Could be the sweetest revenge.

To Andrew Kearns

I didn't have a strong *personal* goal in life,
Until you filmed your next great adventure.
As a photographer,
I felt lost without purpose
Until I saw you embark on something so wonderful and great,
I felt compelled to stay alive and witness something worth seeing
before I die.
In some moments, I wonder if you saved my life-

You made me plan for my next greatest adventure-
Iceland.

Allow Yourself to Be Seen

I used to wonder why, when I felt sad,
I clung onto three movies that always made me feel better-
Not because they were hopeful,
But because they reminded me that someone out there could understand,
And that although secrets are kept,
Some will reveal themselves to be
The true heroes of our stories.

Learning to Love

There's a moment of realization
When you learn to fight for yourself,

How I Learned to Be Grateful

Whenever I feel ashamed that I am not being as grateful as I should be,
I think back to when I said goodbye to the person who filled my life,
And how my last word was nothing but my hand in her hand,
And a kiss to her cheek to silently say,
I will see you again.

Always Moving, Never Stopping

The repetition of life has not crossed my path-yet,
But when it does,
I will still be ahead of it,
Only glancing back at it in the distance,
And then winking
To say,
Have fun trying to keep up.

Burn Brighter Than Ever Before

Laying in a bed of flowers,
Drenched in kerosene,
Her fingertips like matches ready to spark,
The same way they snapped for the blooming season,
Calling life to its cycle,
Like she was Mother Nature herself.

A Letter to Poets, Rappers, and Artists with Bigger Struggles

Do you ever feel guilty
For trying to create something for yourself,
When you feel your story is not worth telling, compared to someone
who had it worse?

Do you think your words are worth less?
Not because someone else deserved the fame,
But because it was never yours to take in the first place?

As I try to empathize with your pain,
All I can really say is-
I'm sorry for what has happened to you.

To the Poets Who Inspire Me

When the *Door* opens to the *Princess Who Saved Herself from the Witch That Didn't Burn,* I watch as she sips her *Milk and Honey* and gazes down upon *The Sun and Her Flowers,* As if she was among a *Sea of Strangers* to whom she couldn't relate.
She sits there-an observer;
A listener.
I make a quick *Note to Self.*

When You Realize You Eat Now

I just ate veggie chips,
A chicken sandwich,
Some more veggies chips,
And then some organic popcorn,
But the organic doesn't matter-
That was just what we had in the cabinet.

Oh, and I washed it all down with sweet, creamy coffee.

Hearing this, some will say I was high,
Some will say I just ate what I had because I was broke,
Others will just assume I was bored and had nothing else to do,
Others will ask "why?"
And I will be the only one left surprised that I actually ate in the
first place.

Thank You for Surviving

Today I stepped on the scale
And saw the same number-a little more, actually,
Except this time,
I lifted my shirt,
Joyful that I didn't look worse.

Trust Me, I Remember

I remember all the wrongs I've done.
I mean, it's not like you'd let me forget,
But did you know that my mind is a broken projector?
The same images will flash in my mind,
Without your voice there to guide it.

Why It Didn't Work

Each story that I told,
You thought I used it as an
excuse,
But really it was a reason,
Because the hidden truth was,
I didn't love myself,
And that's why I never could have loved you.

The One

Let someone love you for who you are now,
Not who you will become later.

I Think This Could Go Somewhere

I started to notice that,
As I imagine myself as a character in others' poems,
I think less about her,
And more about you.

How to Live Life Right

As I sit here twiddling a lighter between my fingers,
I start to wonder,
If a lighter can make a candle burn so bright,
And that candle eventually dies,
Would it think of its diminished life,
Or how it brought so much light to others?

Live in the Now

Don't let the future
Blind your sight
Of what's happening now.

Planning for the Future

I bleed from the nose during new season beginnings,
And I used to feel hopeful that death was approaching,
Pressure and painful thoughts draining from my head.
But now it is a reminder that our existence is limited,
And I wonder, how will I leave my legacy?

To the New Emerging Artists from the Aspiring Professor

Invest in being an artist-
You will not regret it.
Even if no one else supports you,
Know that I always will.

For You (One Last Time)

I still miss you.
And
I still love you.

Renaissance

I think I just rediscovered
the artist-
within me.

Taking the Next Step

What art do you create
When the suffering ends
And the healing begins?

Hello Again Best Friend

Dear Friend,

The last time we talked, we found ourselves engulfed by the trenches of the deep sea where there was no life raft to be found. I remember drowning, and how the taste of the water finally got too salty for me to handle any longer.

That's when I came back to you.

I never had someone so open to hearing what I had to say. *Everything was okay.* It seemed as though the rocky cliff was a leap of faith and no longer a fall to death. When I returned to the ocean, I was prepared. I brought my own lifeboat and found the edge of the world. It is not as lonely as you think it would be, out there drifting into the unknown of what is to come. I know you must be thinking *Why a life boat instead of a raft?* It is because this time when I trek back out to the dark blue sea, I wish to carry as many people back with me.

PERSONAL NOTE

After a trial and error of therapy, I decided to give it one last try. The following year, after I completed this book, it was clear that depression and anxiety were severe symptoms that existed, but what was concluded was that they were symptoms of a broader disorder. In June of 2019, I was diagnosed with Bipolar II Disorder, which allowed me to visually see the patterns that I have lived through for the past ten years of my life.

It was after this diagnosis, that I was able to start treatment with a combination of therapy and medication to help subside the effects of the disorder and learn coping methods to help with the daily disruptions that come with having this in my life.

Before I began any sort of treatment, even before I sought counseling, I had a strong stigma against therapy and medication as to the fear of possible consequences that could follow, and the history of past patients that stated that medication was ineffective to their treatment. As somebody whom was able to eliminate bad habits over the course of many years of tolerance, I can vouch for the use of therapy and medication, and now I seek restoration in the betterment of my health and my happiness.

Most importantly, live your life with what will make you the happiest, because we are only guaranteed our time in the present.

R E S O U R C E S

If you or a loved one are struggling with mental health, substances abuse, or physical abuse, feel free to contact the numbers below:

DEPRESSION HOTLINE: 1-352-771-2700
SUICIDE PREVENTION HOTLINE: 1-800-273-8255
TREVOR LIFELINE: 1-866-488-7386
24-HOUR DETOX REFERRAL: 1-800-449-3008
TREATMENT SPECIALIST:1-866-644-7911
NARCOTICS ANONYMOUS: 1-800-397-2333
NATIONAL SEXUAL ASSAULT HOTLINE: 1-800-656-4673
NATIONAL CHILD ABUSE HOTLINE: 1-800-422-4453
NATIONAL DOMESTIC VIOLENCE LINE: 1-800-799-7233

A C K N O W L E D G E M E N T S

I'd like to thank first and foremost, Kallie Falandays; my editor. You have stuck with me from the very beginning, and have seen this in its most RAW form, to its beautiful transition to completion. I literally cannot thank you enough.

To Kory Kirby, who did the book layout and cover design for the book: I truly am enthralled by your ability to produce such amazing content. I am truly blessed to have had you by my side, and my oh my, was it an honor to interview you for my podcast! You are a great inspiration to live life to the fullest.

To Kaitlyn Hebden, your artwork blessed this book with such beauty, that its visuals truly represent the epitome of my writing.

To Ramelyn Ballon, for your beautiful cover art.

During these hard times, I was struggling very much, and thanks to my other family: Jose & Gabriella Lopez, I was able to rely on some amazing people to help me through trying times while I recovered.

Lastly, to my Nana, who made me into the person I am today. I love and miss you everyday. I think you'd be very proud of your grandchildren's accomplishments.

And thanks to you, the reader, for joining me on this journey.

A B O U T

Dune Stewart is a multi-faceted freelance photographer and writer, striving to produce work that resonates with people around the world. He recently produced a photo book titled, *Premonition*, that surrounds the stages of the COVID-19 experience in the United States, which is apart of his upcoming solo show exhibition. He graduated from Arizona State University with a BFA in Photography. He is also the host of the podcast, *Do You Like Ice Cream?* – An Artist Podcast, where he interviews artists across the globe, to pinpoint their uniqueness in the multitude of artistic crafts. His other interests include: voice acting, Twitch streaming, hip-hop music, and filmmaking. This is his first published poetry book.

UPCOMING:
Cactus Sweater – a poetry book of love and heartbreak. TBA 2021

FOR MORE LEARN MORE ABOUT HIM, VISIT:
dunestewartphotography.com
facebook.com/dunestewart
instagram.com/dunestewart
twitter.con/dunejacob
twitch.tv/R2DUNE2
www.youtube.com/DUNEJACOB